Freedom *From* Grieving

PAIGE D. LEHMANN

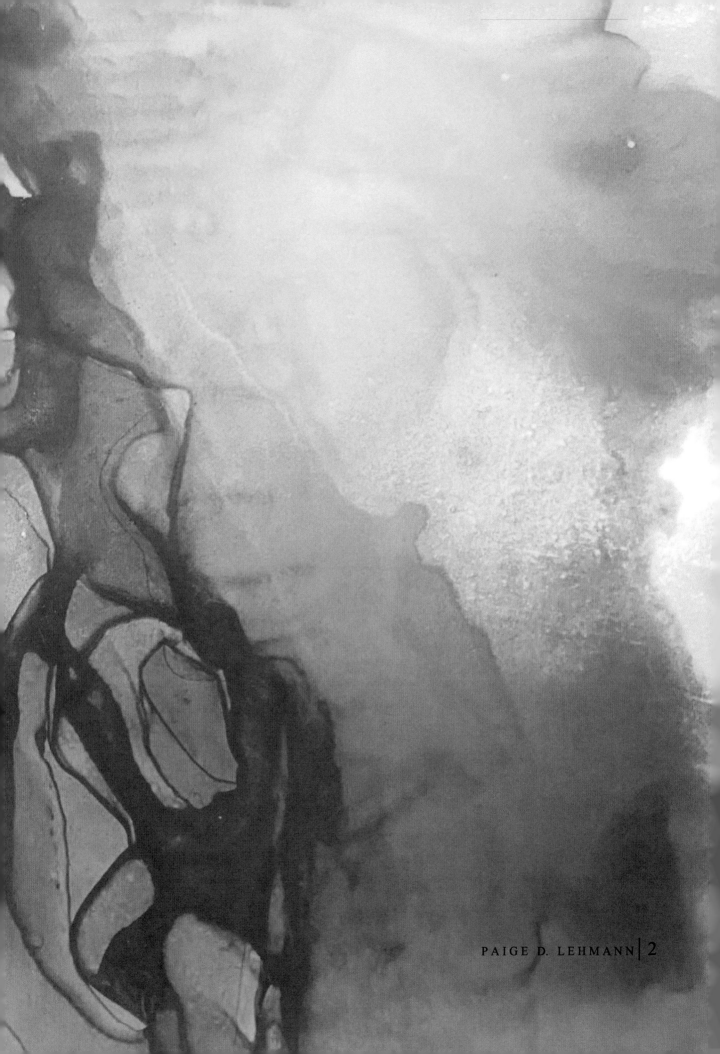

Freedom *From* Grieving

———————————

Poetry and Artwork Series (2019 - 2021)

When Love Calls
Freedom From Grieving
Momentum
Wellsprings

PAIGE D. LEHMANN

ISBN: 9798835287116

DEDICATION

———

To my Beloved One:
You say I am your muse.
It is impossible to unlock without you.
I love you forever, Chris.

CONTENTS

————

INTRODUCTION

———

This book is comprised of four sections: *When Love Calls*, *Freedom from Grieving*, *Momentum*, and *Wellsprings*. Each section holds a different perspective on how I personally relate to love, grief, God, myself, travel, and people.

Within these pages you will find poetry, pictures, and abstract visual art. Although I create with specific subjects in mind, my hope is that you uncover your own stories and interpretations helping you better understand the world within and around you.

When Love Calls is exactly that. We explore love with a capital "L". What happens when that *much bigger* Love reaches out? We hear God is Love. Could this be true? If we replace "God" with "Love", could it be that love is a *who*?

Freedom from Grieving captures my personal grieving process. This section includes images from the *Freedom from Grieving* exhibition featured at the Mesquite Arts Center in 2021.

In this section, you'll find a winding path within each piece. The paths' initial debut forms within the first painting and dissolves into the last. This process moves from a discombobulated "unknown" regarding where to go or what to feel in relation to our loss and moves into the explosion of the heart. From there, the path reveals possibilities for healing and ways to pick up the shattered pieces.

Freedom from Grieving is inspired by my dad, who, during our conversations growing up, provided special insight and wisdom regarding the nature of grief. In these conversations, he considered the complexity of grieving. How grief is comprised of emotional tidal waves all requiring attention and care.

We've all felt the waves of grief in one way or another. I have found that each time we deliberately choose to integrate the healed understanding of our loss into our deepest innerworkings, our strength and beauty reaches new heights. Although we lost something or someone, we also learn how precious life is. With new understanding, we launch into the present and embrace everything life has to offer. In my experience, this is freedom from grieving.

Momentum is a series of poems written from 2019-2021. A very interesting period in life where we all grew weary of participating in major historical events. These musings are not necessarily in any order. They simply represent the growth I experienced over those few specific years. This section also includes poetry and images of commissions during 2019-2021.

Wellsprings is a book of travel. These poems, photos, and commentary amplify moments where I experienced an overflow of joy. I realized gratitude is the lens for beauty. You'll find most of these poems are inspired by France, the place where I met myself…and where God met me.

Welcome to the beauty my eyes have seen.
The world is worth loving.
3:16.

Part I.

—

When Love Calls

PAIGE D. LEHMANN

When Love calls
Will you be seated in the past?
Wrapped up in the fast-track haze
Names stacked against *names*
Reflections called you?

When Love calls,
Will you see Love's hand reaching out?

Love is calling-
Do you hear?

When you know the sound of Love,
There can be no mistaking.
No questioning.
No wondering about the bonds of the past
Telling you why you need to move
Fast
Out of the way,
Out of Love's way,
Into another phase of darkness
Which overtakes.

For the symptoms of Love

Continue to shove

Old voices of knowing

Fakers foreshowing

Where your breakthrough is showing.

Light is light.
Dark is dark.
Love is Love.
The rest can wait.

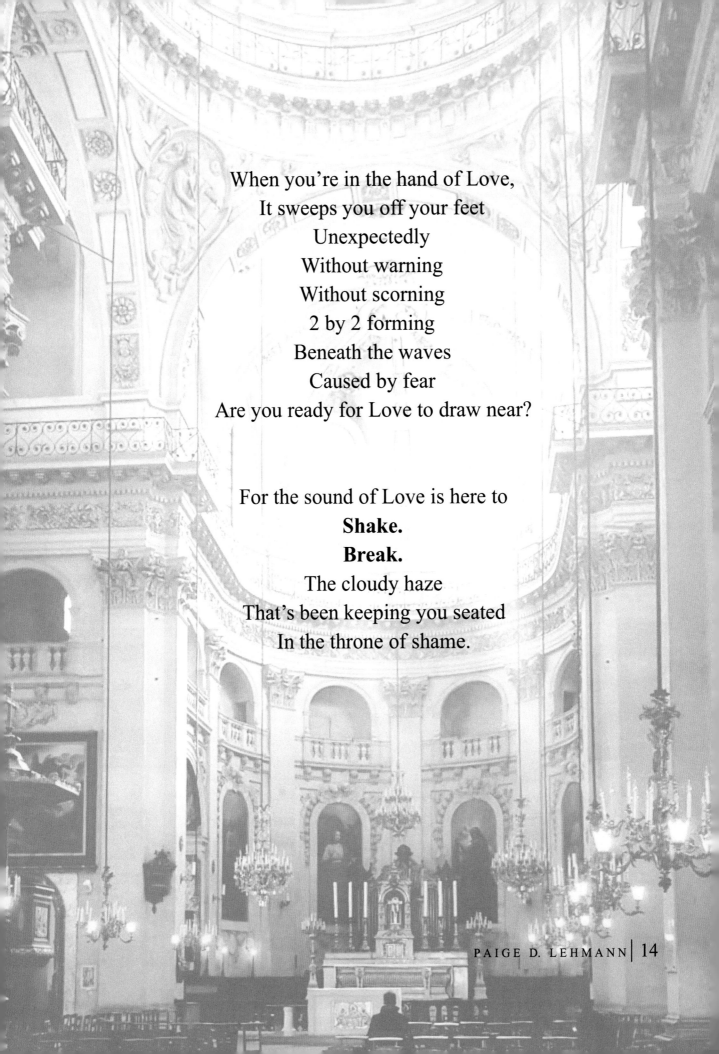

When you're in the hand of Love,
It sweeps you off your feet
Unexpectedly
Without warning
Without scorning
2 by 2 forming
Beneath the waves
Caused by fear
Are you ready for Love to draw near?

For the sound of Love is here to
Shake.
Break.
The cloudy haze
That's been keeping you seated
In the throne of shame.

What if the guilt robbing your joy
Had a time ticking end?
And regardless of how you felt about that
The guilt is ending now, within.

Regardless of the truth of the past
Of endless warning,
Scorning,
Shaming your name,
Flaming your shame,

What if there was *freedom in the heartbreak*?

Of cracking, breaking, billowing clouds
Demoing the giant lots of cemented block
Built up by the shock of where you've been
And where you *know* you need to go...

And then Love becomes a whisper,
A listener
Your all-time defender
Of that which hinders you.

No longer held by space and time
Because Love has its very own rhyme
With the rhythm and beauty
Love calls you near
And holds your ear
To tell you what's
Sheer.
Fake.
Nonsense.
Mainly resting in our own thoughts
About ourselves,
And about this night.

And Love will
Tell you
How your future is brighter than the night
Brighter than what's in sight
Brighter than what you think is your right
Brighter than the lone star resting alone in the night sky
You're *brighter* than the obvious sigh flowing from the lips of your
unfulfilled strife.

Love,
Love,
Love,
Is chasing after you
Whether you like it or not.

So *when* Love calls…
Are you ready?

For the night is befallen
With a twinkle of light
The dawn of day breaks the haze

So *when* Love calls,
Don't stay ashamed in the backdrop
Of your worried life.

Let Love call,

And break the night.

JE SUIS NE EN L'AN [...]
[...] JE MESURE 5 METRES DE CIRCONFERENCE
[...] METRES DE CIRCONFERENCE DE [...]
[...]
UNE VALLEE ARIDE ET [...]
[...] LE CONSEIL GENERAL DU GARD
PASSIONNE PAR MON AGE ET MON HISTOIRE
M'A ADOPTE AVEC DEUX DE SES CONGENERES
J'AI ETE PLANTE LE 23 SEPTEMBRE 1988
JE SUIS FIER DE PARTICIPER AU DECOR
PRESTIGIEUX ET NATUREL
DU PONT DU GARD.

Part II.

—

Freedom From Grieving

PAIGE D. LEHMANN

SECTION 1:
THE UNKNOWN

THE
UNKNOWN

Upwards slope: unknown.
Upwards means to leave what's known.
Upwards glances not.

Look back, become stone.
Look back, my glass heart will crack.
Look back, speckled notes.

Unknown: where I go.
Unknown: how will I go there?
Unknown: where to go.

To fall means I *fall*.
I could fall all the way down.
I refuse. Onward.

PAIGE D. LEHMANN | 27

SECTION 2:
THE EXPLOSION

THE
EXPLOSION

A single atom in the heart
Compressed and then separated
Creates the explosion of a lifetime.
One that cannot be replicated.

Toxic fumes revealing
Concealed wounds
The firecracker of the moment
Keeps us re-living the moment.

Over and over again
The path truly begins:
Freedom from grieving.
To leave the fumes,
One must walk into the new.

Just as a single atom held in the heart
Compressed and then separated
Is never forgotten,
So the weight of grief
Forces us to seek relief
Freedom from grieving
Is walking, moving, loving, and leaving.

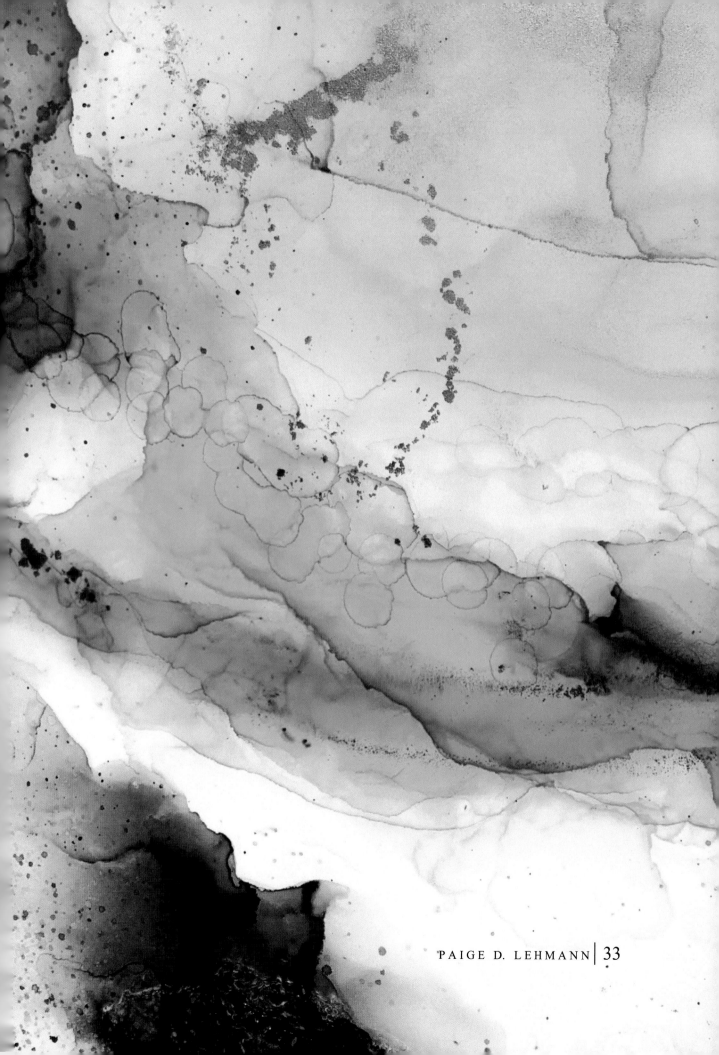

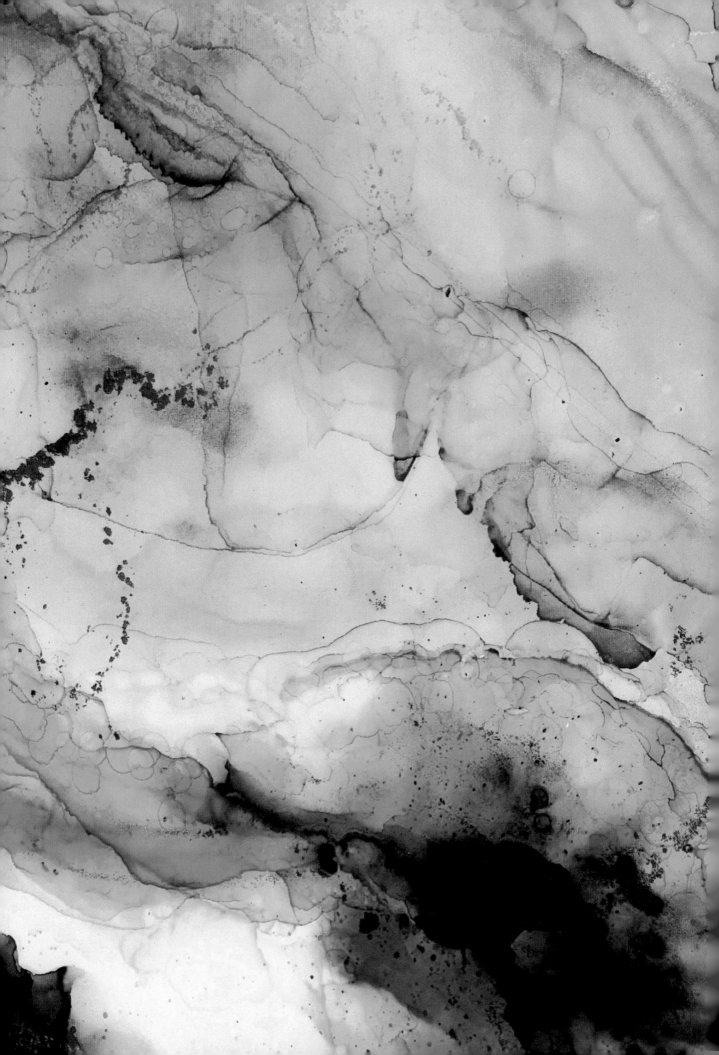

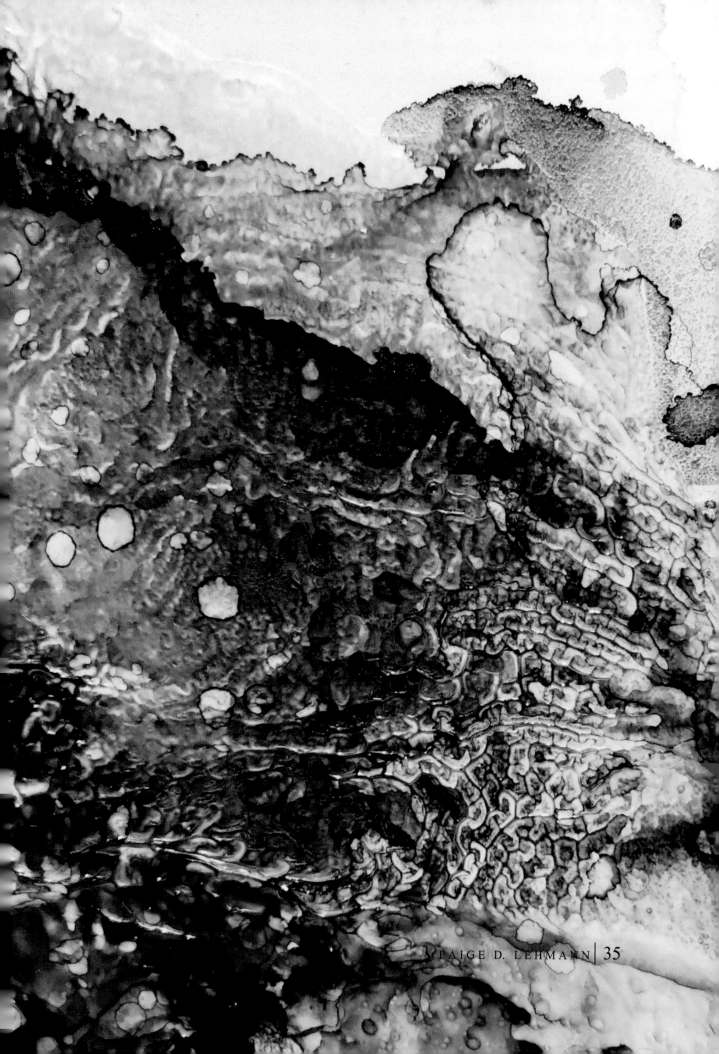

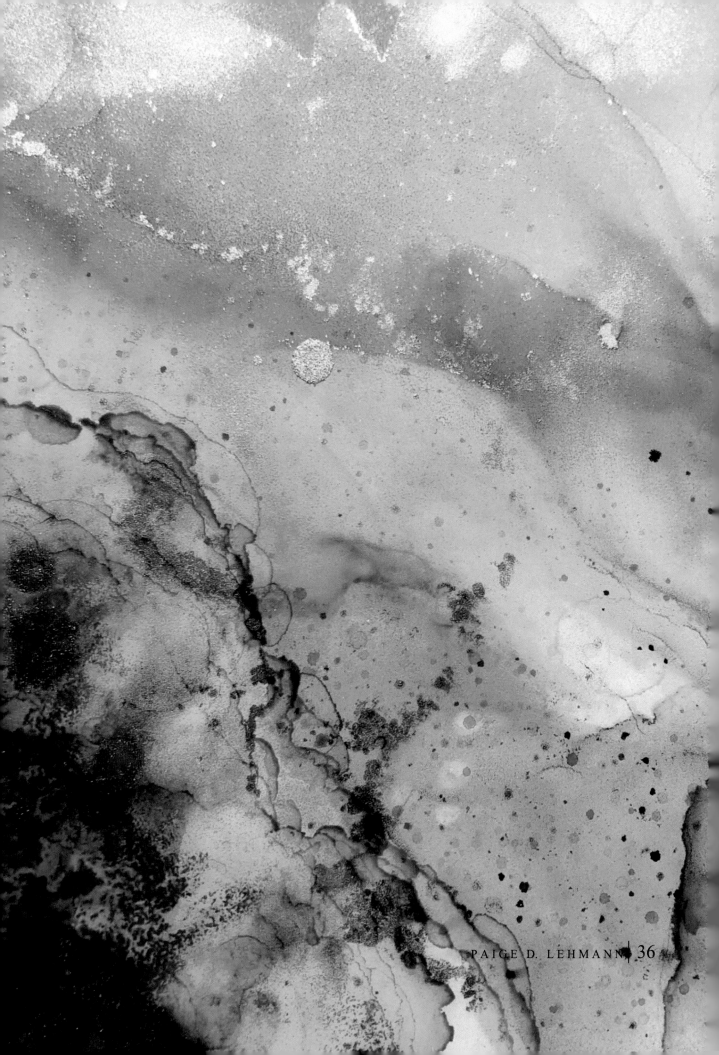

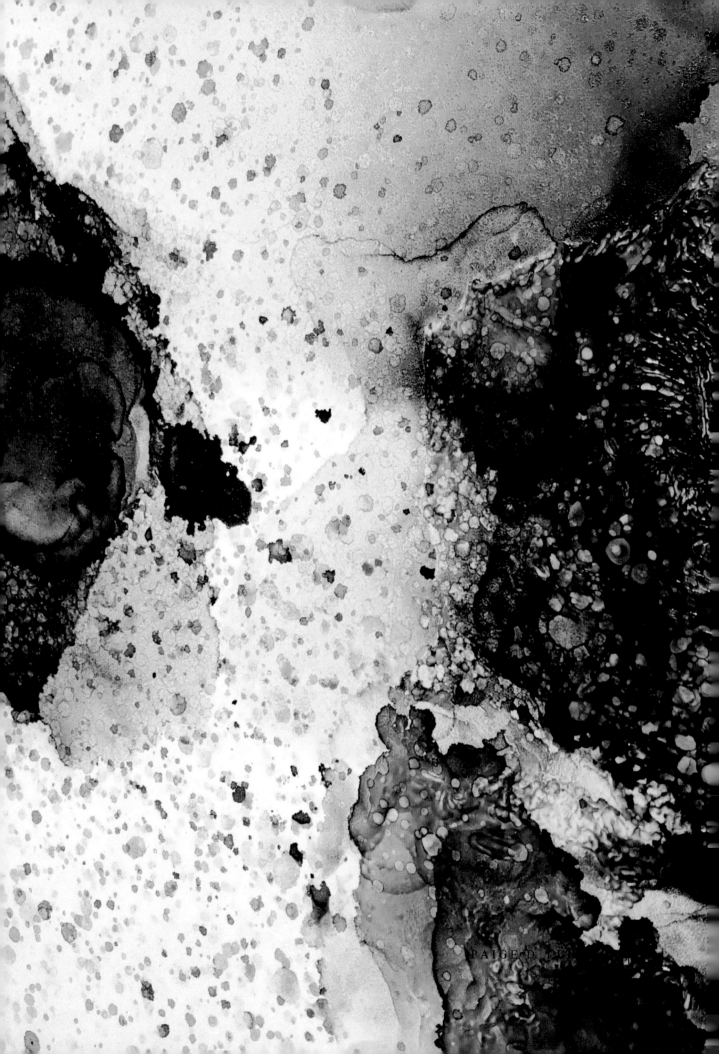

SMOKE & FIRE

———

Burning questions catching fire
Forcefully asking what could have been.
What was lost outside also steadily burns within.
Deep fire, lines of illuminating smoke only to
Rise up higher painting those vast veins within our internal sky.

As we walk, our questions emerge rooted in "why".
With each raised question is an equally raised choice:
To stay on or to move. We must always make the choice.
No matter up or down,
Left or right, side to side…
…no matter which direction we choose, even at our best

Smoke begets smoke
We're still lost in the fumes.

Just as certain as a warm summer night
Shares its heat with a blue moon,
The answers we find to why
Rarely hold any meaning at all.

Most of the time it simply is, just like the blue moon.
Thus for us, it is certain:
We must walk, and walk again
To satisfy then leave behind
The ancient coals and toxic fumes.

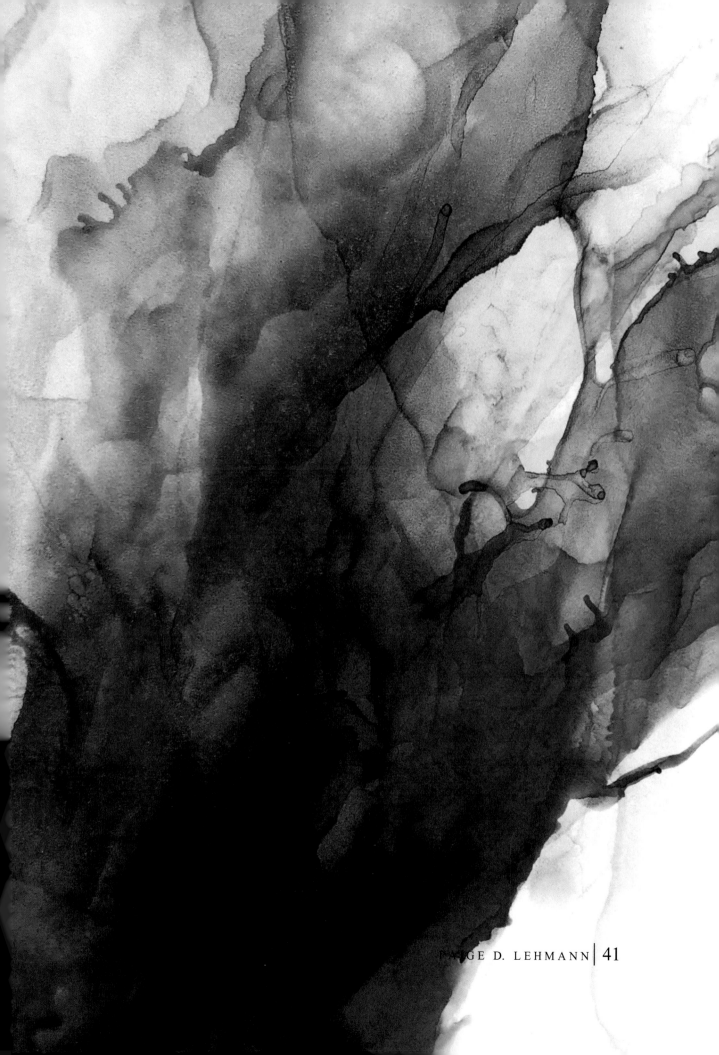

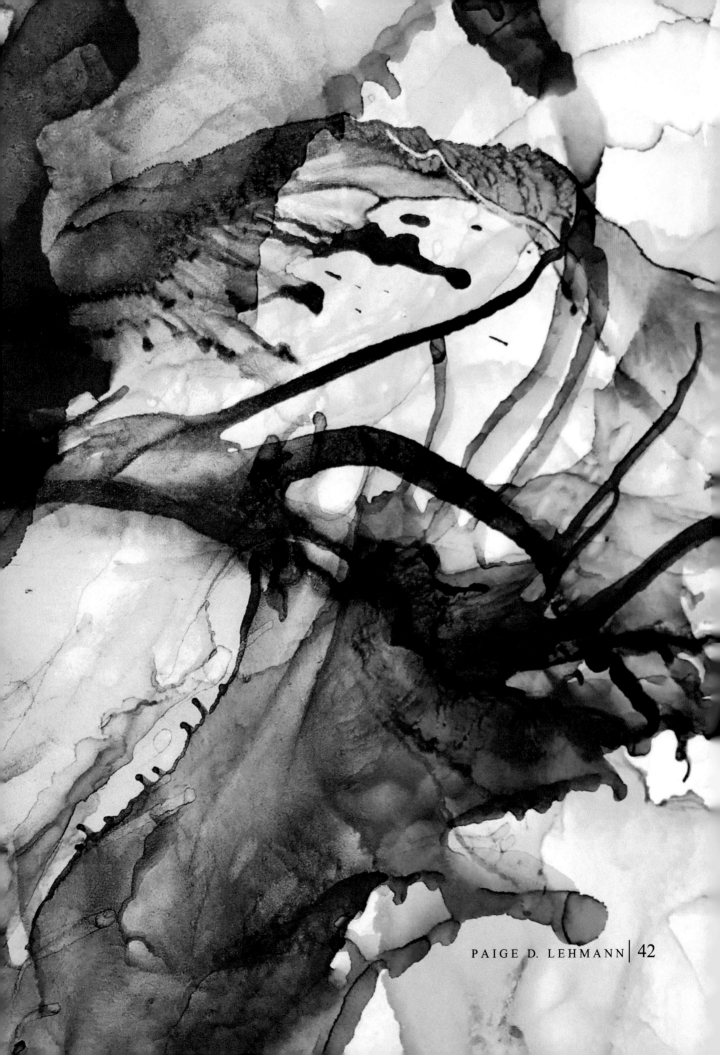

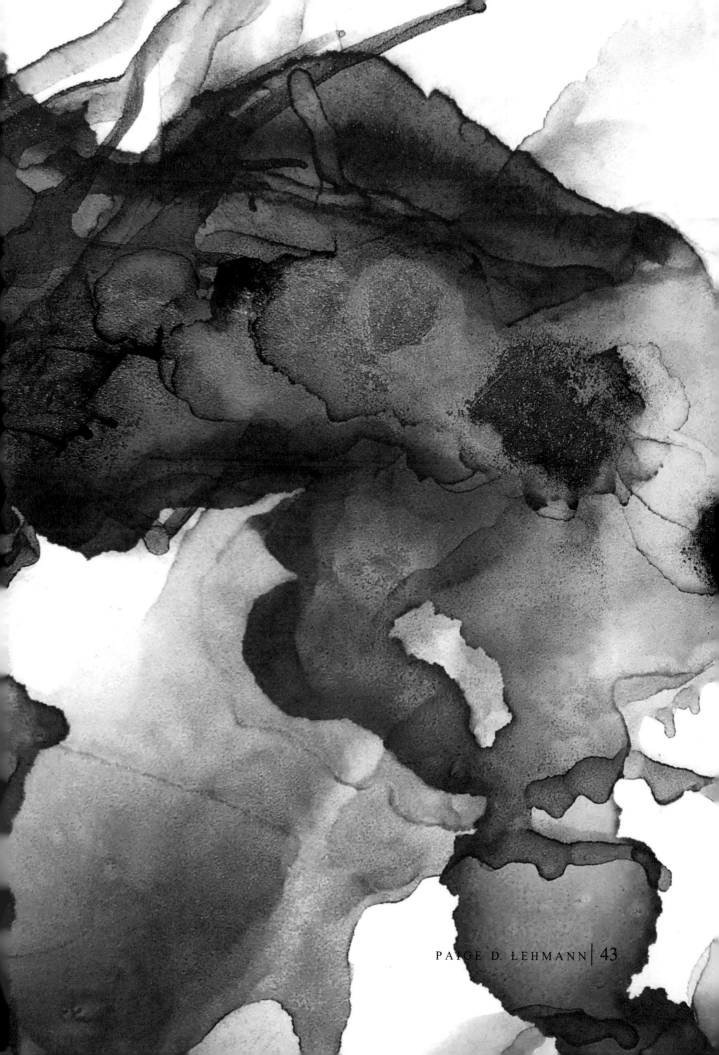

THE OASIS

Scorched earth.
Rarely heard.
The oasis reaches
Bright, deep pigment
Into scorched earth
So we may dip

And take a drink.

The oasis is
A silent invitation
Wading,
Waiting,
Intentionally wandering
In and out

Brushing against our rocky shore.

The veins of burnt thoughts
Rarely understand.
They consider the oasis
A mirage or simply unfair.

The oasis moves in
Waves upon waves
Inviting us to drink in full:
So take a drink,
Settle down,

And repair.

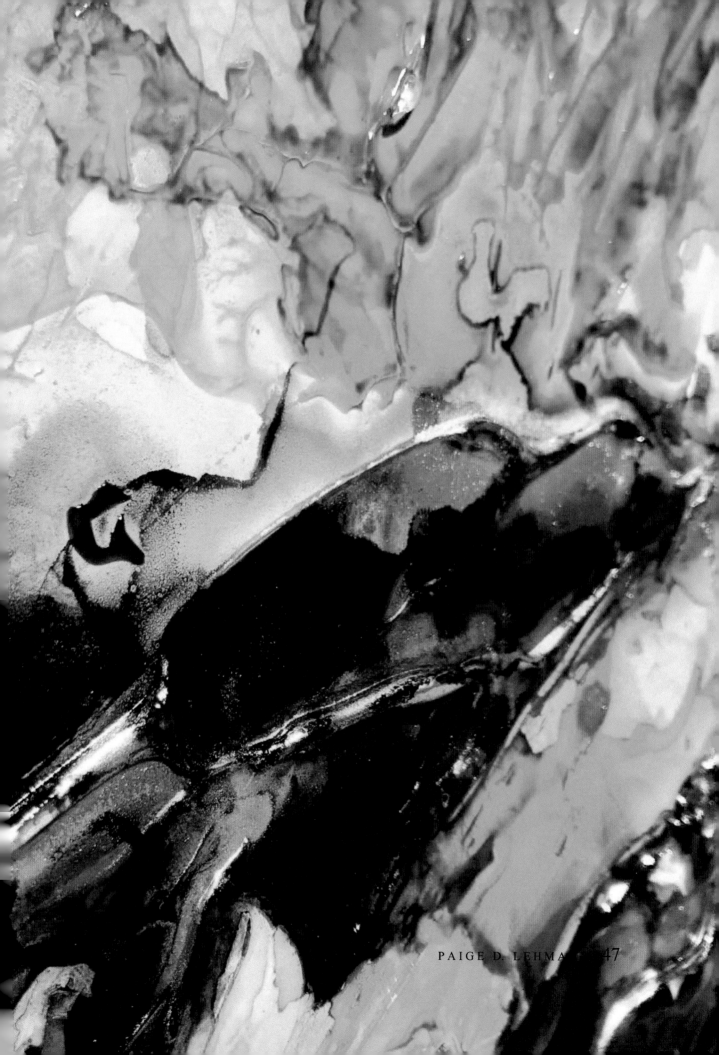

PAIGE D. LEHMA   47

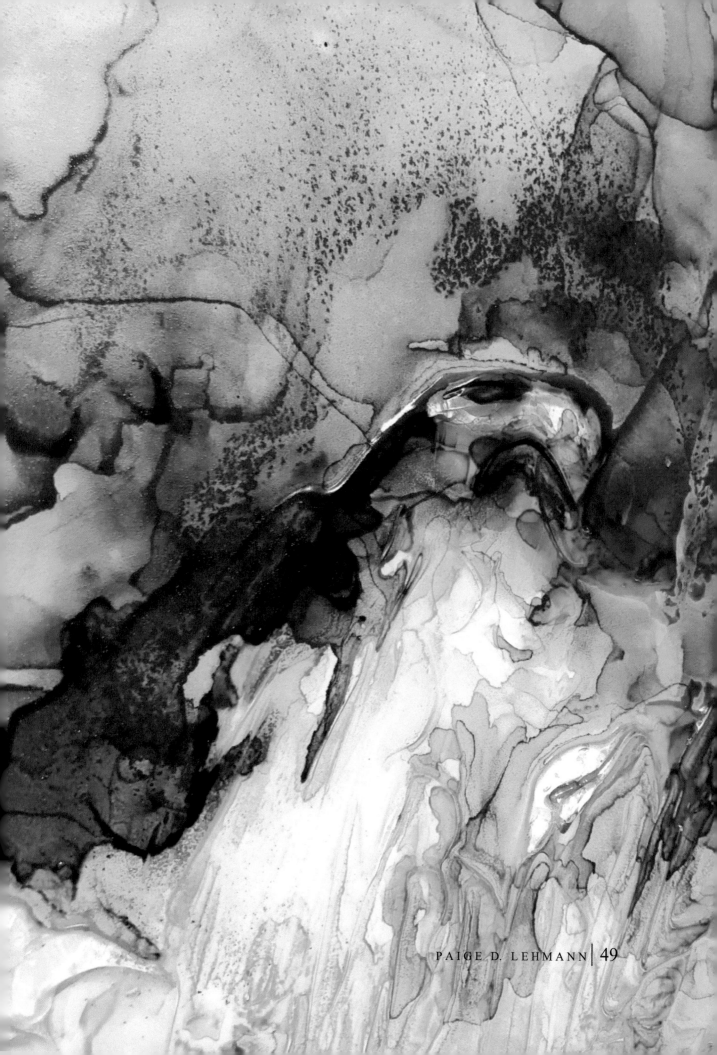

WHEN DARKNESS MEETS LIGHT

Many standing paths of grief
Mixed with sadness,
Anger,
Certain defeat.

In the background
We see darkness
Clouding to meet the light.

Do we know the old story?
Or do we forget it to forgo it?

When darkness met the light
It could not understand.
It could not overtake.

And if we step away from our
Fearful, dreary, melancholy way
Despite brick-by-brick,
"Protection" being taken away,
We see that light has eternally won
Booming in the deepest darkness.

Yes, even *that* darkness:
The kind we call our own…

When darkness met the light, the old shattered and broke away.

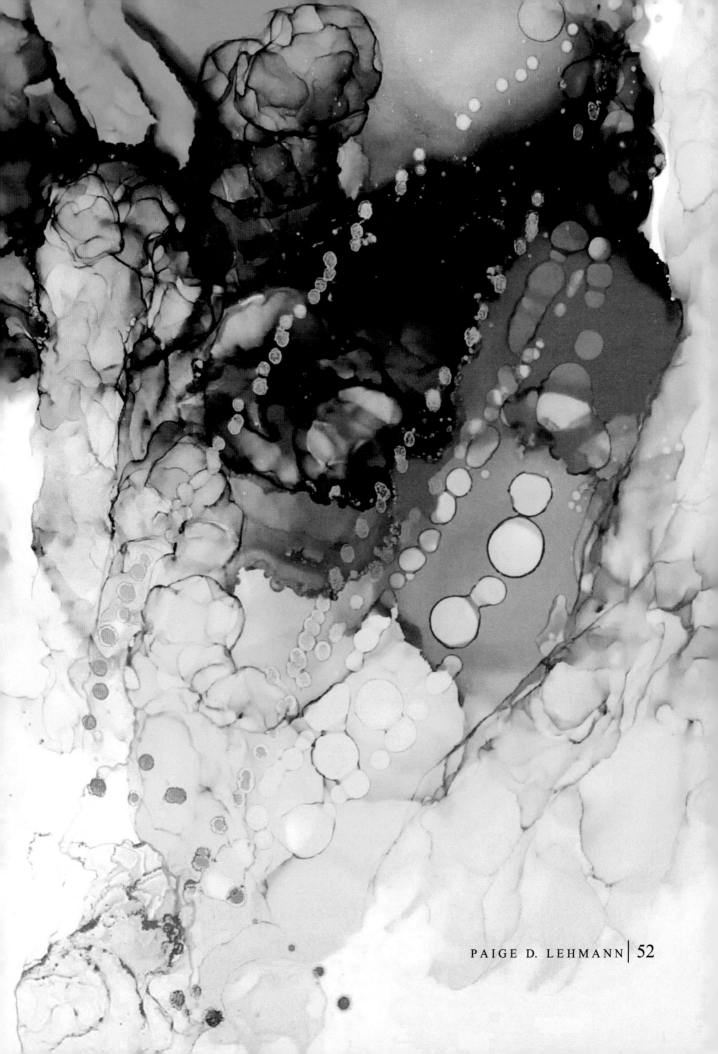

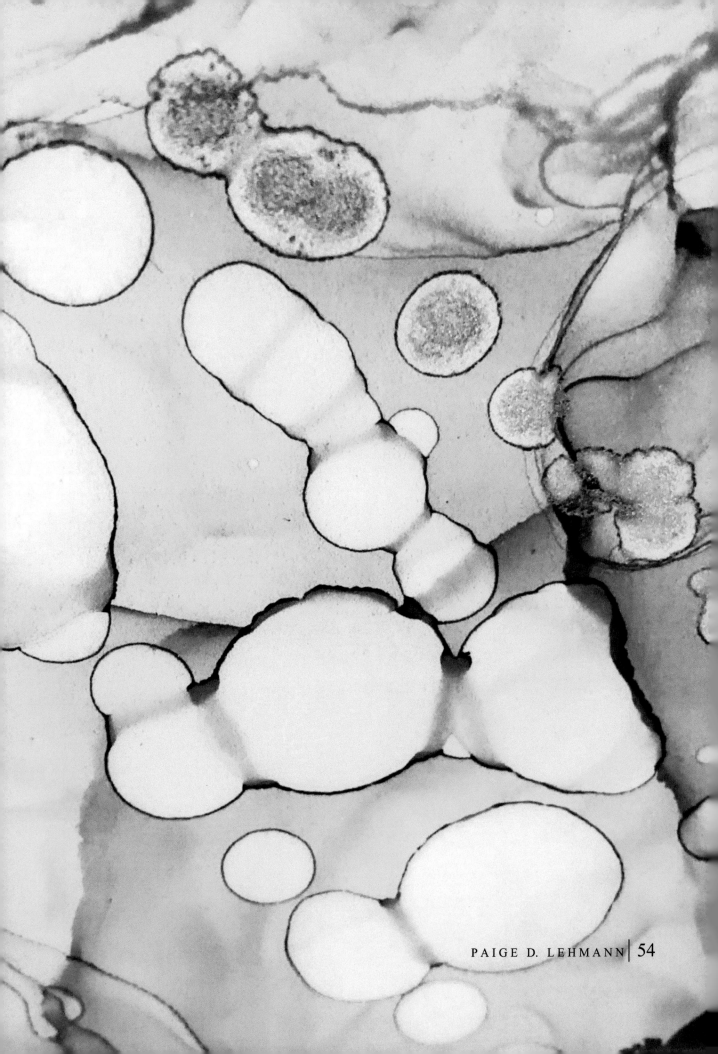

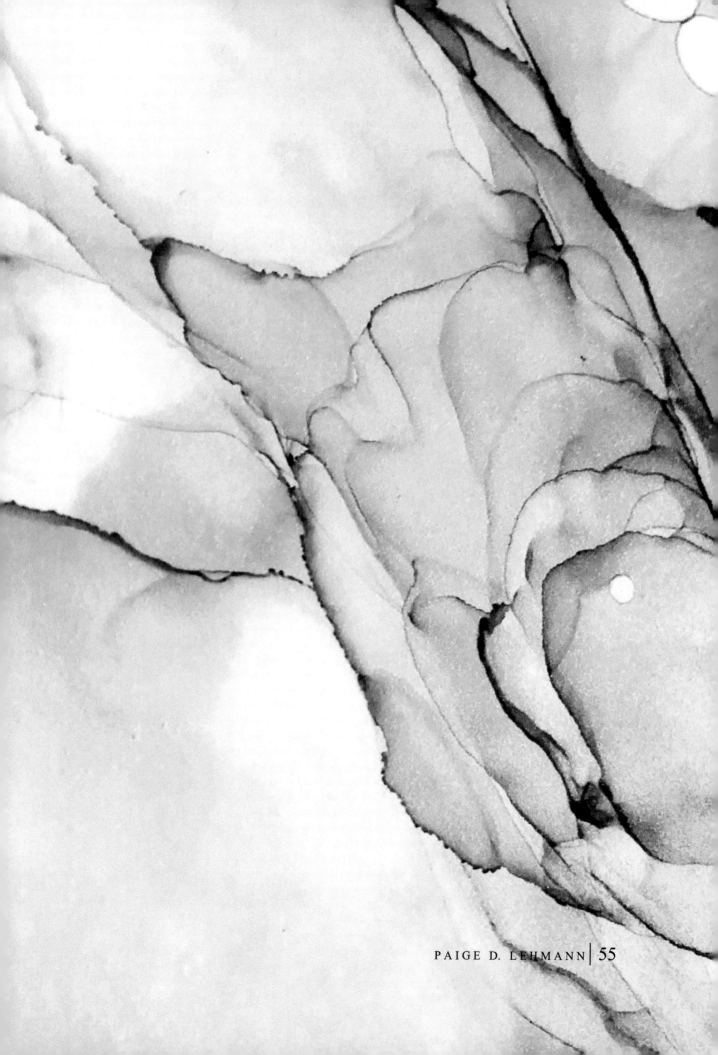

SECTION 3:
THE HEALING

VALVE REPLACEMENT

If this shredded valve stays
I will not stay.

The weary parts of grief
beg defeat.

To remain small,
broken,
unable to function.

The path becomes brittle
and I find myself open
to whatever healing means
and whatever healing brings.

Another day is more than
a day.

A new day
is a new way
and I am happy to say:

despite the grief,
I am here to stay.

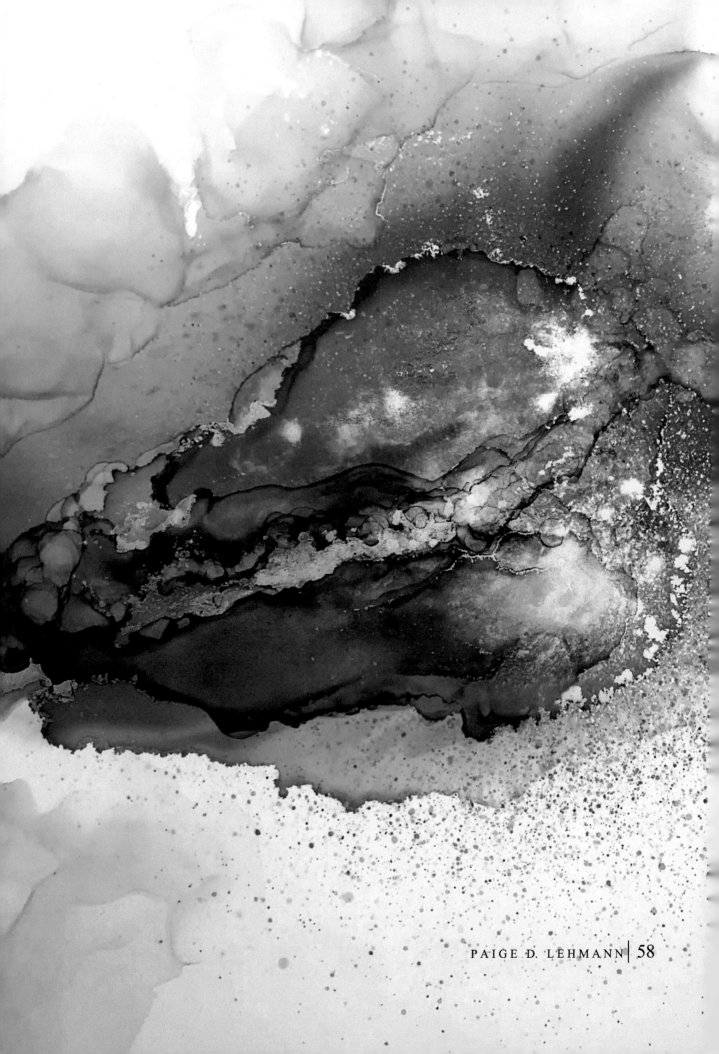

PAIGE D. LEHMANN | 00

ELECTRICITY

———

Bright.
Between two phases:
the beginning,
closer to the end.

Electricity.
Between two poles:
shock and relief
life and grief.

one may not hold the other.
with a flash
they are connected
Then promptly disconnected
by the weight and bold entry

Of electricity.

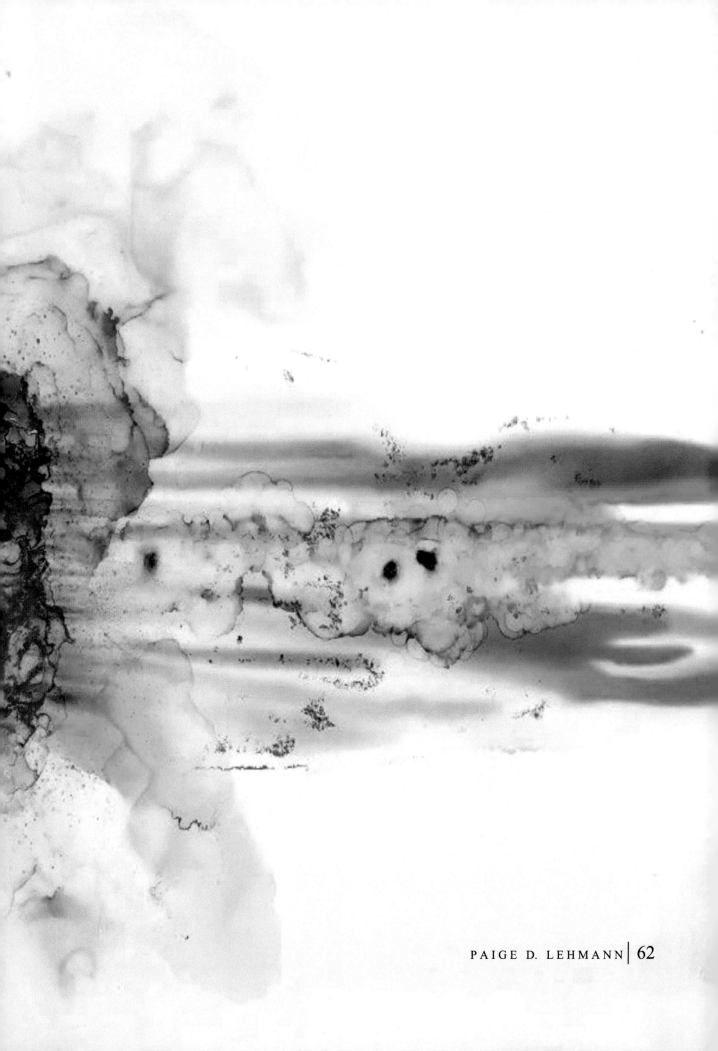

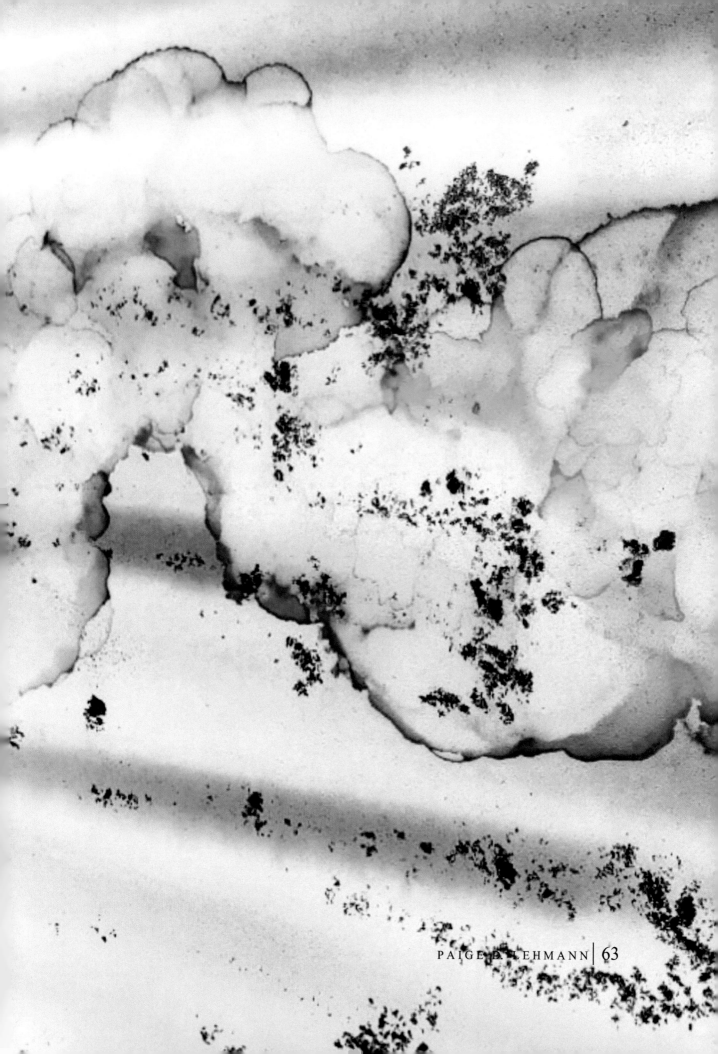

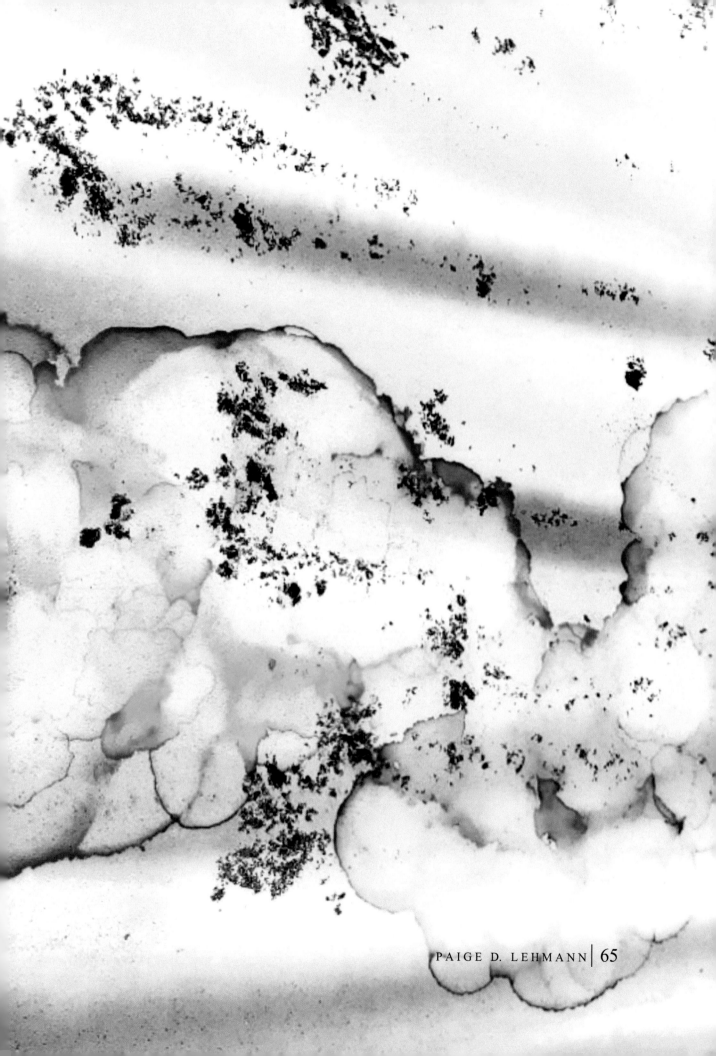

JOY

—

Melancholy grief no more
As I learn to sing new patterns of
Beauty, unexplored.

Though grief has marked me,
Left me tattered and torn
I heard a new song left for those unadorned.

So I found it,
I sang it,
And pulled myself into joy

Instead of imploding
I exploded
A new sound of joy.

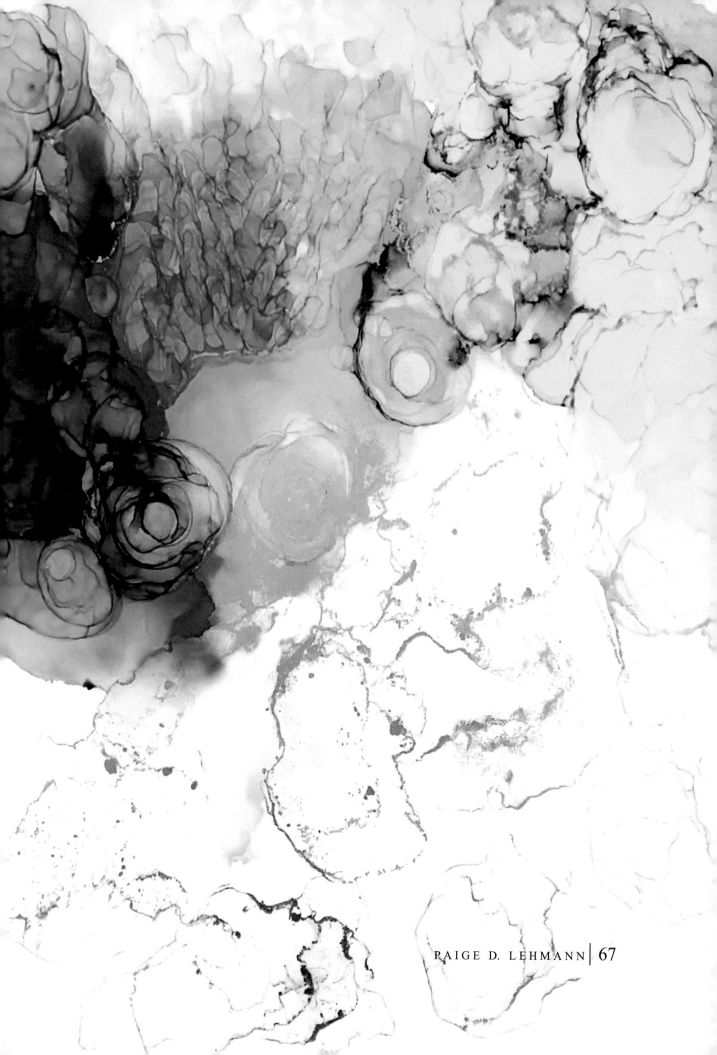

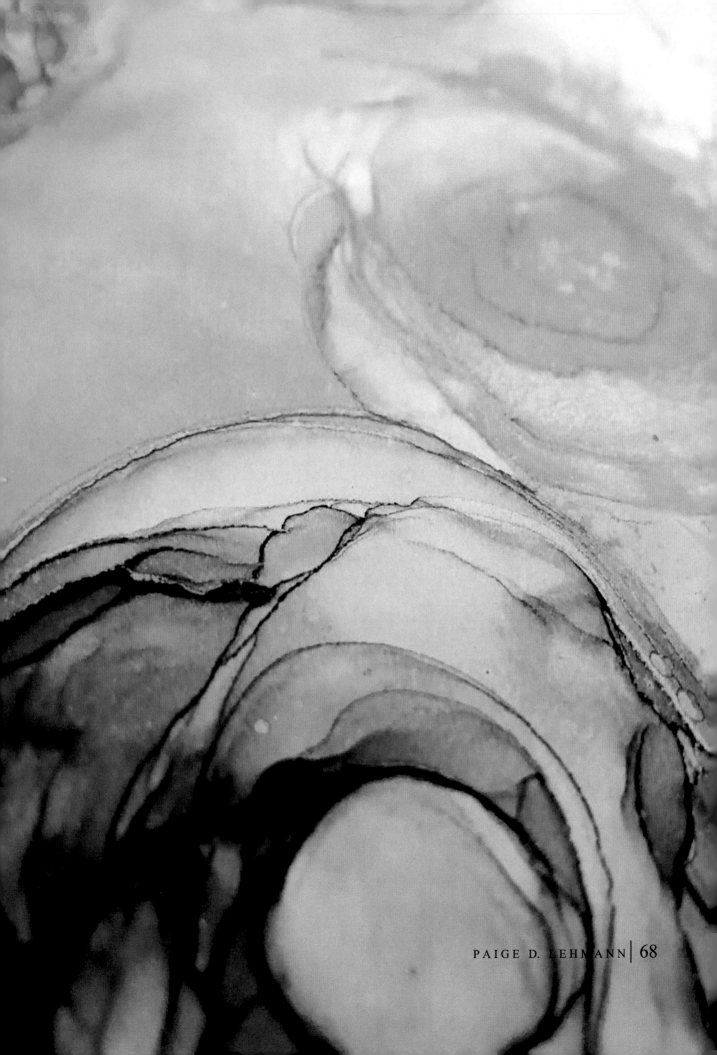

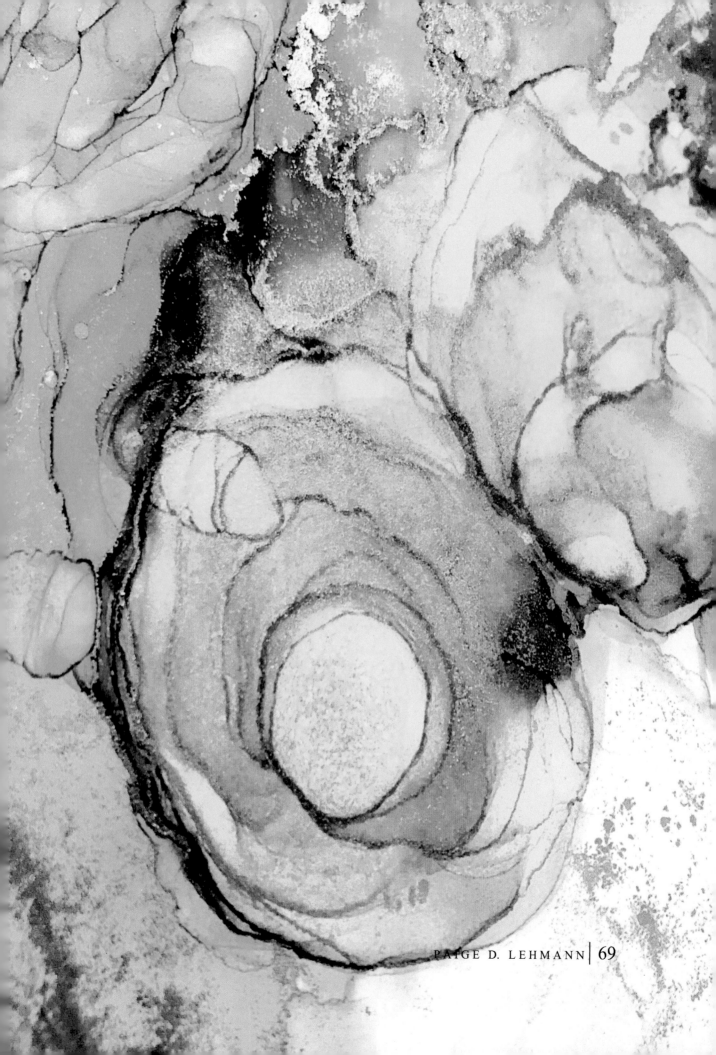

THE EXIT

Colors bleeding into new shapes
A path entirely ending
Blending itself into waves unending
Signaling the bright new day.

As the sun rises
I am left without questions.

It simply is.

And with this,
I move in a new, bold, expectant direction.
I have held the hand of grief.
Walked in deep waters,
Felt little relief.

Yet despite this,

I forever choose to heal.
So one day,
As we walk

I am able to hold you:
Fully, freely, peacefully.

This, I believe, is freedom from grieving.

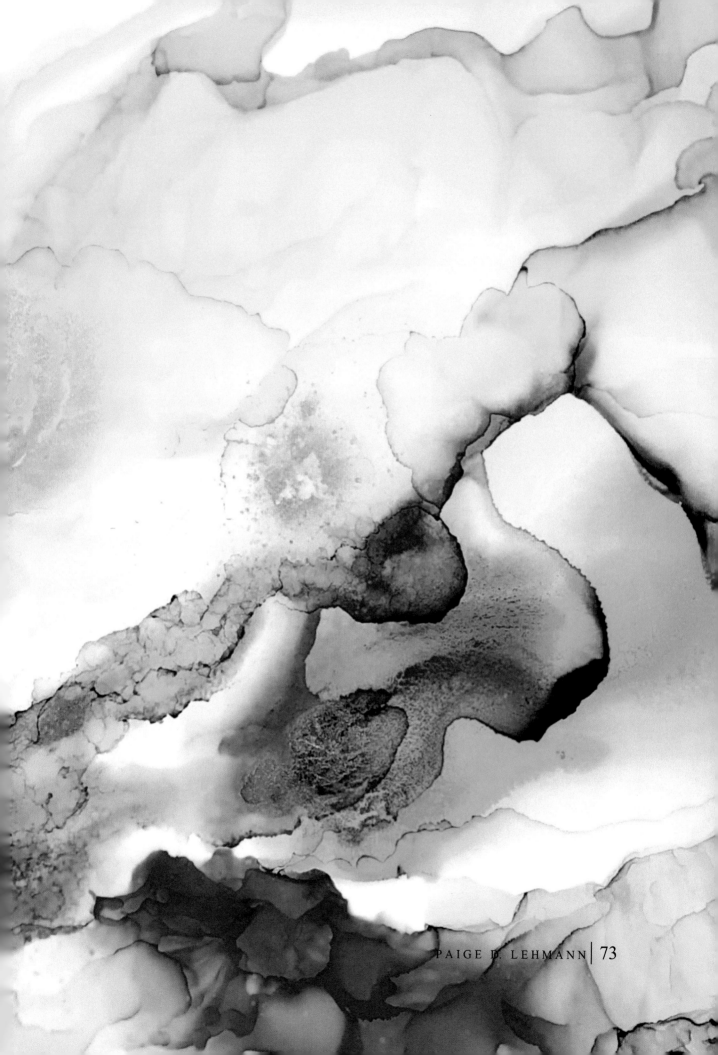

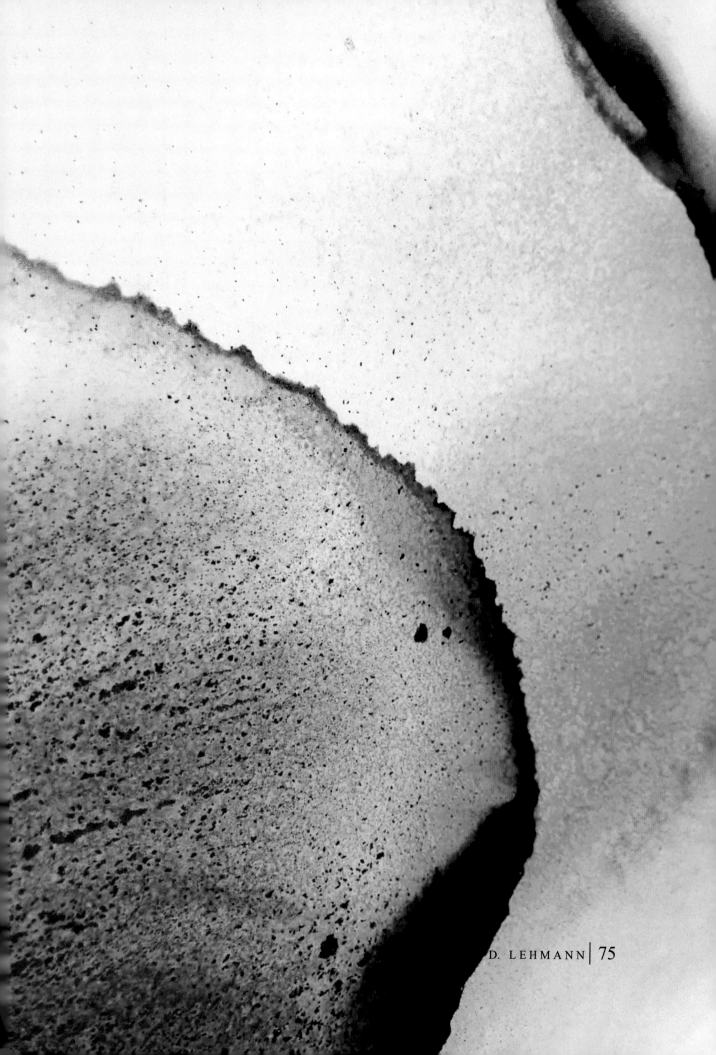

D. LEHMANN | 75

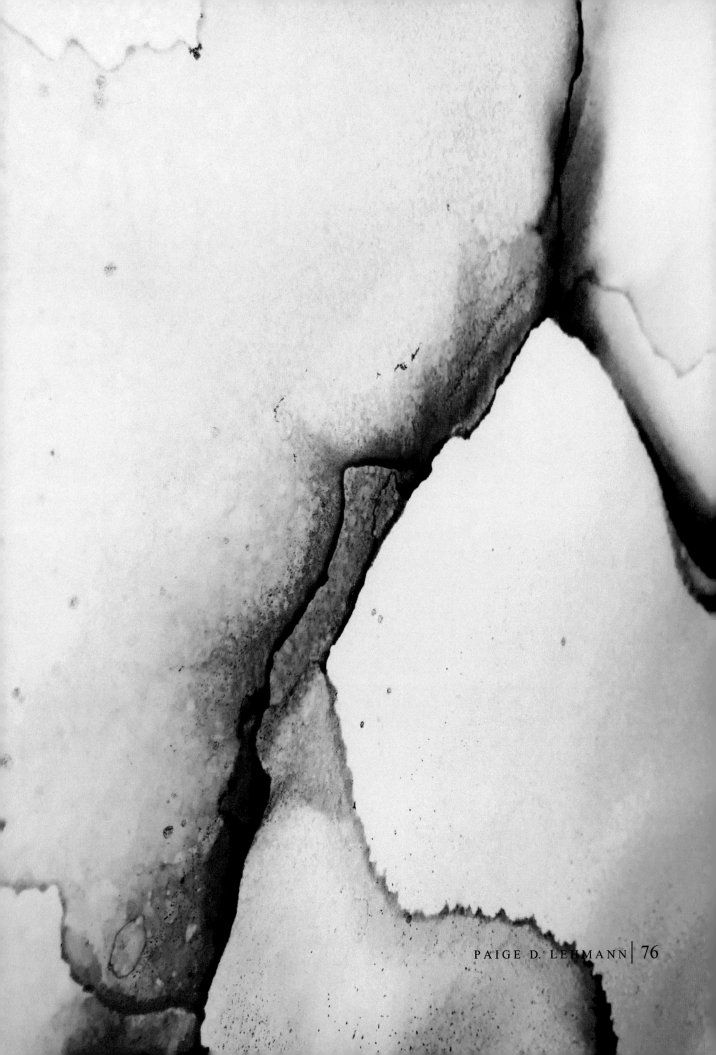

PAIGE D. LEHM

Part III.
Momentum

A Collection of Poems: 2019-2021

PAIGE D. LEHMANN

i.

May your eyes know
love
in this time of need.
May your ears know
love
despite what you believe
about the world as you know it,
you don't have to hold it,
the depths of despair
is already broken.

May your song be reached,
even if you don't believe
the sky is for you,
I pray you learn to believe.

May your eyes know
love.
May your ears know
love.

May you know:
You
are
made
for
love.

ii.

like dewdrops in the morning
are my simple words for you.
poetry unraveling,
beat 1
then meets
beat 2.

my lips are drenched with dewdrops
sweet dewdrops just for you,

no malice
nor bad intention
are these dewdrops made in silence

ever learning
ever yearning
to see your thoughts take flight
from the world as you know it,
let nothing be old from it

may you grow into your own
as a dewdrop in the morning.

iii.

Forever

What does it mean?
Sidewards eight
Like this: ∞

Our love is shaped like a sideward eight
Wrapping into itself
Moment by moment
Perfumed by the sincerity of
Respect for you
Respect for me.

Forever,
We are bound.

I love you

Is how we begin to count it.

iv.

You knock, moment by moment
You knock
You seek
You find
You unravel
You ask again
You seek again
You find again
You unravel
You share
You ask
You receive

In this way,
You are going to break and shatter old ways.

v.

I don't know about you
but i want to do more than merely make it through

life on fire
love's desire
let me be

on fire
on fire
on fire

for what I know is true:

you,
you,
you,

I love you.

vi.

however humble the calling looks
the calling does not stop
calling,
searching for you.
as you wade in
bitter waters,
the calling moves you
to brave deeper
oceans...
those whom you have
never met before.

Yet you take out your hands
and reach into that great unknown
to be delightfully
and frighteningly
trapped in what you know is true:
the calling is no longer calling.

Nor does it have to.
It doesn't want you.

It sees you.
It found you.

vii.

Take kindly to those
around you
even if their truth
is an untruth:
Grief bears weight on
their mouth
while Grace grips
with might

to your ears.

viii.

Because I love you

My life wouldn't be complete

Without you healed...please?

ix.

Gold speckles infused
within our heart valves;
moving within channels
we never knew.

Once we meet them,
see them,
breathe them,
all becomes new.

X.

The rose,
fragrant and deep,
lights up the world around her.

Forward she speaks,
delicate she thinks,
and more than ever
not her beauty,
not her body,
she, her whole, is seen.

xi.

Dark sentiments borne
from isolation
spring forth
when distance pushes
the clouds of disdain aside.

what we felt inside
was never a lie

simply a misalignment.
as we skip into the
truth
never fast-forward
never re-wind

simply press play

and watch

as all

aligns.

xii.

In the unraveling
comes the exposure
needed to move forward
no more ordering
what is next
the rest
lies in someone
Else's hands.
and within a
moment,
suddenly,
peace,
now

we're at rest.

xiii.

Jump into creativity
launching beyond
what is
and run into
what may be.
through
explosions of color
comes
waves of laughter
from
fear breaking its grasp
of iron clasps
on the wrists
of your soft heart
asking,
always,
to be set free.
and even more,
always
asking

to be seen.

xiv.

If the sky could crack
leaving a shattered
window in the sky
breaking barriers
of sound and light

if love truly came
in it's own name
and ripped,
tore,
forever,
the curtain
between
purity
and
man

who am I
to rest in insignificance?

xv.

Who am I to be in vain
At the hand of comparison?
Wrapped in bitter wonder
At the fleeting thought of
Someone else's life?

Who am I to test the
Waters of vengeance
Only for the taste
Of melancholy freedom?

Leaping through past regrets
My life grows older,
My way becomes narrow
As I make my way to the banks of
Saving Grace.

All that I am,
Wrapped in a moment.

D'un seul et même souffle.

xvi.

When love stepped in the water
And dipped down
So did the sky

I tried to deny it
Yet many years later
My eyes bear witness,
They know:
The sky meets the deep.

No line on the horizon.

This, I cannot deny
Even if I try.

xvii.

Deeper, deeper, deeper we go
One goes up,
The other knows.
Eyes fulfilled
Hearts will hear
the crying out of a joyful tear -

A tear of knowing,
A tear of showing,
A tear of kindness,
A tear for what's near:
Hearts showing
Eyes glowing
Smiles knowing
Only flowing
Into what is new:
Life renewed

Life,
Life,
Life,

Renewed.

xviii.

Upstream flowing
against the grain
rowing and knowing
I have an internal guide
a gift given
since the start of time
or so it seems
if I understood time.

There's a time
to go against the grain
a time to know,
let go,
flow,
be alone.

a time to be together
a time to show
a time to step away
a time to row

these are a few things
I learned
in the undertow.

xix.
Despite the thorns
    Around the truth of
       Your love,
          Despite the pillars of clouds
          Shrouding your name
      First I heard the depths
        Reach its hands
          And cry out
       At the sight and sound
        of who you are.
       And then I saw
          Who I am resound
            As you reached out
          Asking, always, for the
          Strings of my heart.

           Gently pulling
          Those thorns away
          Pesky and deep,
          Then reintroducing
            Re-tuning
        Each string of my bitterness
          To the harp of
           your peace.

xx.

in the beginning
was the word
or at least,
we know
a sound was heard.

in my beginning
i said one word
in my "yes" to you
our firecracker
our sound
was all we heard.

When Joy Bursts Through the Cracks

This next painting and poem is extraordinarily special to me for many reasons. It is inspired by Mesquite, Texas. Somehow Mesquite is larger than life while maintaining that small town laid-back-kinda' life so many of us enjoy. I am grateful to say I found a home in Mesquite. The friendships made, stories heard, and the changes I've seen over the years is beyond belief. Every gift given to me in Mesquite holds a unique experience that no other place could provide.

When Joy Bursts Through the Cracks is inspired by two different events. First, the project "Restore the Joy" Mitch Mitchell (from Sound Alarm Studios - go check him out) and I executed together from 2018-2019 with three incredible young musicians from Mesquite ISD. With that, this poem is also inspired by the Front Street Station groundbreaking event in August 2019.

During the groundbreaking event, we gathered downtown behind the historical buildings parallel to the rail-road tracks that put Mesquite on the map. Each one of us took a shovel and pierced the ground, together, in a prophetic heralding, stating: this land is now opened, and will be different from here on out. Upon striking the earth, it felt like ideas released from the ground into clean air. History was broken open. Such a simple act made a profound statement in my world. To my surprise and delight, this piece was selected and featured at the Front Street Station Grand Opening event several years later.

Mesquite, thank you for being who you are.
I love you very much.

When Joy Bursts Through the Cracks

———

We sometimes do not recognize
When joy bursts through the cracks.
For we usually notice cracks
Lining older streets,
Older buildings,
Older things.

But we know:

Century-old prayers have spilled into the concrete of Mesquite.
A history is kept there: wide, enduring, and deep.
In the depth and in the steep
We continue to leap
From one epoch to the next
And here we are, moving into the next.

I'll tell you:

I watched as the community gathered around
To break the ground
Passing out vials
So we may carry pieces of
Uprooted grass, roots, and concrete
To remember as we leave.

Although that's not everything in this timeless soil,
It certainly felt complete
As I held earnest prayers,
Ardent history,
And felt unfading joy release.

When joy bursts through the cracks
Nothing can stay the same.
For once joy is felt, known, and seen
History is honored history
And joy is left on repeat.

COMISSIONED
PIECES

The Nature of Our Love

———

The nature of our love
Could only be told
By an unending sea
Brought, developed, and seen
By both you and me.

Spiraling through tunnels of light
Illumination is simply our right.
Built into the fabric of our everyday lives
Can the nature of our love be found.

We move through rivers of grace, everyday.
From bank to bank
Are the tangible traces
Of our not-so-distant past
Resting in residue we choose to see.

This is the nature of our love:
Ever-climbing.
From one blending sea into the other, you see me.
Where do I end and you begin?

Beloved, your sea is one with me.

Santa Fe

I went to Santa Fe
To taste the land
And paint for a friend
As distant clouds
Peek over the peak
Of mountains and valleys
I remember
My time with her,
Singing.

Layers and Traces

———

Every line you made stretching across horizon after horizon
scratching old ideas bringing forward the new.

Those lines you made: built in. retraced.

Every touch, every hint, every golden tint touching that trusted
dawn you always knew was worth tasting has arrived.

Every terrain you walked, every word you spoke, every moment
you've taken to glance at that promising horizon,
built and cumulated, leading you to this moment of now.

Of dreams becoming things: lasting, promising, lining up.
Matching all your heart is after.

As layers are held,
                opened,
                        trusted,
                                known,
                                        your sweet heart shows
                                        and never grows old.

Convergence

Convergence, it seems…
Two ideas
Separate themes
And when they reach out,
Touch,

Beauty shocks the old scene.

But before Beauty can
Make her way to the stage
There's a humble act calling:
To deconstruct and reconstruct
What we've been told about now

and hereinafter.

The baton we were passed
Half broken, left open
Is the same one we use
So those before us can trust-
Yes, we are ones to relate to.

Yet ideas never rest
They can never abuse
Unless one keeps their eyes open
Searching to lose

The breaking wave
Against the rocky shore
Is the one we all know:
Old ideas broken open

The beginning of hope.

Whether welcomed or not
New ideas are now open
Dressed in white,
Here she comes,

Beauty is the explosion.

Vapor

—

I heard that life is but a vapor,
A wisp in time
A subtle rhyme
And we were meant to be happy
During this time as vapor,
Briefly,
Before returning to the author's dust.

If my life is but a vapor,
I'll tell you what I'm going to do:
I will love you like
2+2 loves
Equaling 4
Because as we know,
This stands without question,
Without a thought,
Without needing to understand.

It simply is.

So it is the same
Or so it will be

As we continue building,
you and me.

Now I have told you
No surprise to you
Now you know how I will use
The vapor and dew of my tiny,
Beautiful,
Wisp of life.

Part IV. Wellsprings

—

Poems while Traveling

PAIGE D. LEHMANN

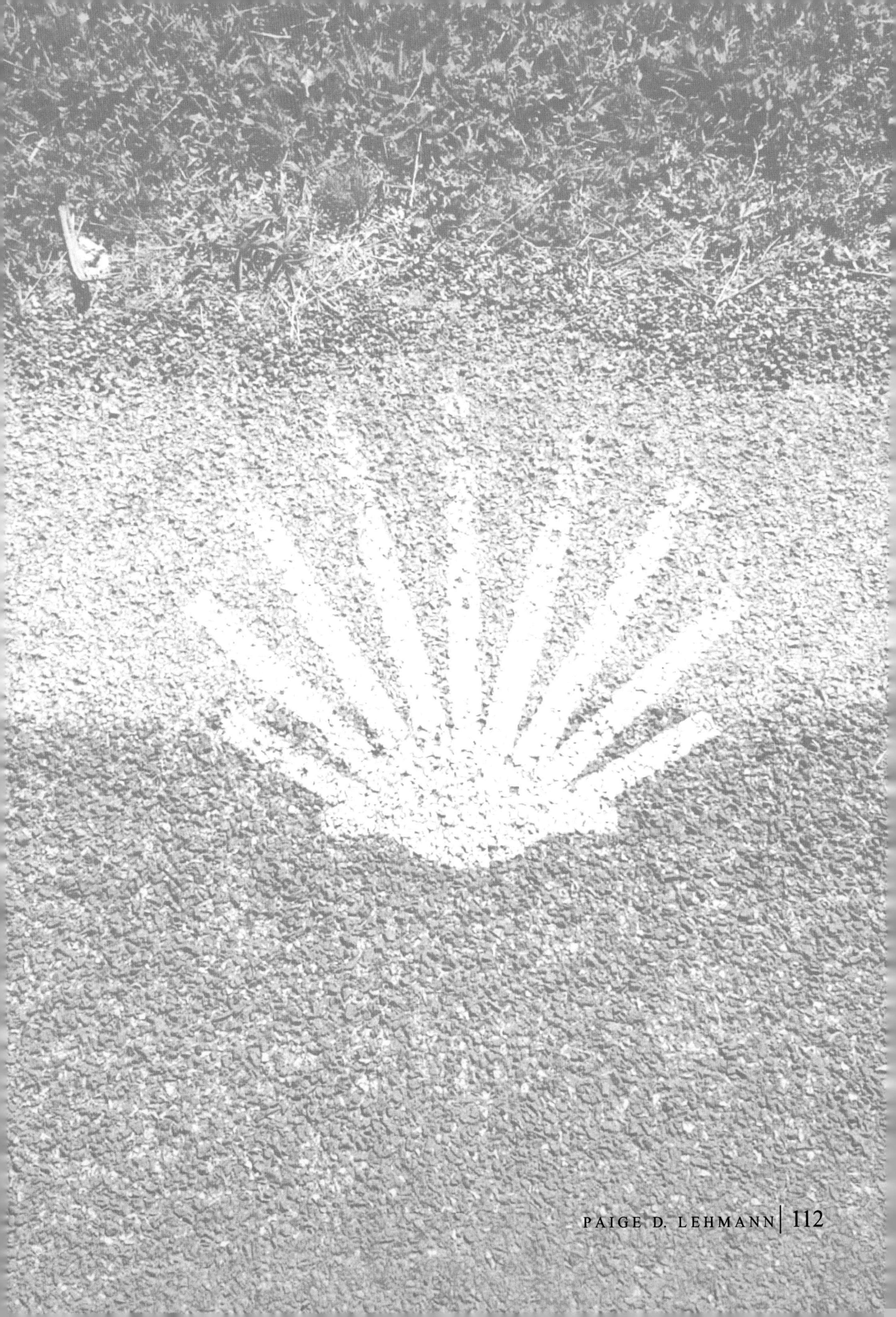

PÉLERINAGE

"Beauty"
announced the mountain tops
majestic and steep,
dipping down, reaching out,
to greet the valleys deep.

I met my childhood rêveries
on the edge of a cliff,
with a croissant in my hand
and volcanic rocks beneath my feet.

I walked on foot through the French countryside:
Le-Puy-en-Velay into Aubrac, to Nasbinals,
as each foot touched the ground,
I watched as the beauty of color met sound.

Ne Crains Pas, Je suis ton Dieu
C'est Moi qui t'ai choisi,
Appelé par ton nom....
rang through my ears
as I walked along the way.

The Way marked with people
all of us, made from clay.

I met cathedrals and people
what beautiful people.
It's a pleasure to meet
to greet
to share
why we're here, most of us...
walking through concerns only God can repair.

I met bookshops and stories
curious quarries
not built by man
nature carved her own stones
she breathed in God's glory.

You could find me
as I walked through the distant past
lightly touching walls
where the great saints passed.

There is something I know:
although I belonged
in those ancient halls
religion called grief
showing and sharing
that in my best try of all
still…

I'm no saint at all.

It wasn't until I stood beneath
arches of green that
I felt heard, seen,
and although I wasn't looking,
heaven found me.

In the vast plains
marked with
speckled gold,
happy cows,
in the vibrant air
lined with wisps of clouds
heaven found me

through daisies dancing with petals of white
french poppies breathing pure air; perfect light
honeysuckle blooming bright white and gold
hills rolling and roaming
the path climbing and winding.

The mighty pine trees' scent
Lined our lungs as we moved.
Deep hues of blue
Blackberries to eat
Pulling each of us from the path

"For a moment. Just one treat."

Butterflies found us
Fluttering about
Sharing that darkness
While chosen,
Is not meant to keep us
We're meant to break out.

From the moment of acceptance
To the very last road
Sprinkled with wildflowers,
Wild goats,
A river flowing,
Guiding,
Showing,
Knowing,
Even if I didn't believe,
I can't argue,
living water dwells in me.

With that age old promise
I was led up those mountains
In the colors of sound
I remember:

> *Darkness, while chosen...Ne Crains Pas*
> *We're all meant to break out.*

This poem is inspired by Le Chemin de St. Jacques (The Way of St. James). I started in Le-Puy-en-Velay, which is a small town with a large cathedral on top of a volcanic outdrop in the middle of the city. By the end of my journey I made a new group of friends, all of whom poured wisdom, joy, and humor into my world.

The afternoon before starting Le Chemin, I made my way around Le-Puy-en-Velay. During my exploration, I crossed paths with a nun who asked me to sing with her. I don't know how I ended up behind the cathedral, or in that situation at all…which, I guess, is the best way to experience life. She handed me sheet music, and I sight read to the best of my ability despite being completely out of practice. I was invited to sing with her the next day at the public meeting for us pilgrims before leaving.

Although I did not accept this proposition out of fear, our group sang what is now one of my favorite hymns: Ne Crains Pas, (Do Not Fear) from Isaiah 43. We sang the chorus over and over again in that stone cold cathedral. Resounding, bouncing notes reflected off the wooden pews, harmonies blending all throughout the space. The Spirit, through its breath and beauty, brought us together in one space, held us, and met us in the sound.

As we walked, I felt like I was getting glimpses of heaven on earth: I knew no stranger. I had no fear. Every single person walked through that land to heal. Some walked for marriages, health of loved ones, grief, family trouble, or needing to "get away". To talk with anyone is to learn about private areas of their lives…something the French people do not easily allow. That in itself proved a miracle.

There I was: walking and yearning, flourishing alongside every living thing, and listening to creation sing.

* S P A R K *

———

I used to think hope was naive
until I found myself on the banks of the seine
touching land where "The Greats" once stood,
Monet met Renoir
and their history still stands.

Taking their pens, paintbrushes, ideas,
I looked around in wonder:
Why these trees?
Why these leaves?
This water?
These stones?
How did *this* air inspire such beauty?
Any other place, perhaps…
Why here?
Yet did I see that?
Suddenly
spark
New eyes. New perspective.

Beneath the willow tree
You could find me
Reading anything and everything.

Hiding within her branches,
I watch as her leaves dip down
Touch
The seine heard her perfect message.
From the language of leaves to the voice of still water,
spark
the ripples rang out.

The wind was no longer wind
as it caressed the trees
inspiring and stirring
branches up, down,
the fullness of movement
spark
each leaf highlighted.

The wind, the water, the trees
they're all God's chosen messengers.
spark
It's an honor just to hear them.
This is how they speak.

So this is why they painted.
Why their brush was moved and stirred.
Monet met Renoir
heard the voice

now history sings.

Message in a Bottle

——

I don't know how I found it -
that bottle approached me.
Of course, while on the banks
of that infamous French river
I would find the glass remains
of a fun evening with a crowd
or tears with no one around.
Regardless of the story,
that bottle was moving
making its way to Paris
floating along without a sound.
Gibran would argue, so would Cohelo -
there's no accident at all
not even this hello
as that bottle approached me
call it chance
call it even
I picked up that bottle
with hopes of receiving
a tiny note
yet note there was none
so I took my pen, writing
what I needed to read.
With the flick of a wrist and inhale I reached
and sent that note flying for *someone* to receive.

BOURBON ST., NEW ORLEANS

———

Main Street:
Where we went walking,
You and I.
Walking,
Talking,
Sharing ideas,
Down Bourbon Street, New
Orleans.

Men in tutus,
A few prostitutes,
Walking,
Talking,
Did we touch a piece of the
Vatican?

Yes.

And naturally,
We ate oysters
Somehow your gumbo is
Better,
Just like your heart is finer
Than the finest soil
Claiming to be the best
Against all the rest
Your heart is a heart of rest.
Next:
Crab legs reaching out of
po'boys,
Police stacked on horses,
Sneaking hurricanes,
And suddenly

It's 2am?

My dad and I visited New Orleans together in 2013. We started the trip early and listened to Leonard Cohen the whole way. One of dad's friends owns an antique store in New Orleans. We paid her a visit. Initially, it seemed we stumbled upon a unique, although unassuming antique shop. Then she led us to the back. We had no idea our visit was about to go from interesting to surreal. She showcased items from events we heard about in history books. There was indeed a piece of the Vatican propped up against the wall. Dad was speechless. She led us further. I was speechless.

Once we got outside (the back door), Dad and I stood next to the road for several minutes. Although we're not catholic, something about that particular brush of our fingers on that wall of history moved him. We stood. Eyes wide and "what just happened?" on our breath.

We ate lunch and walked up and down Bourbon street over and over again. I was under 21 (oops) and he snuck me hurricanes as we walked around. There was so much to take in. There was indeed a man in a tutu. And a few prostitutes.

There was a moment of clarity as well: my dad is a soulful, intelligent, and kind man. Amongst the excitement of the trip itself, glimpses of the things I love about him and the traits he's given me interrupted the present. Oh, the perspective shifts and humor we encounter when we travel.

PAIGE D. LEHMANN | 127

God's Backdrop

Little droplets of gold
opens the heart to what is known:
God's backdrop needs no announcement,
simply a denouncement of fear.

Eyes wide open,
the heart knows it,
beauty surrounding as our faces show it.

Aging lines decreasing to the sound
of the ocean breeze
leading us to deeper waters
known as "we".

Musings in Santa Fe

—

i.
Fresh air filled with sweet pine
Alone in silence
Finding my mind
The past walked by
I didn't say hello
But glance to glance
Both were known.

ii.
Invitation up,
To places I never knew
Engaged through and through

iii.
Palace of trees
A place to be
Creeks and rivers
Dressed better than
Kings we knew
And of course,
When we see
We also believe.

Rejoice

———

aching to be seen
is written inside of me
to know you
and be known by you
without the touch of a hand
nor on the same piece of land
to be known is to stretch out a hand
into places unseen
where I love to be
I dance in the places
of the unseen
opening up
being seen
and when I see you

Rejoicing breaks my mind.

I fell in love with France like one could fall in love with a person: deeply, irrevocably, without fear and with open hands.

It was such a significant affair that I feel like France itself experienced parts of me no human could ever truly observe or understand. There is so much personality, history, culture, diversity, and wit embedded in daily life. I experienced wild internal shifts: no hint of depression, fully immersed in learning, rich friendships, and the full expression of self. Even more, God led me and met me by the banks of the Seine. The ability to freely see beauty, intellect, and the Spirit around me forever changed my brain chemistry.

To truly fall in love eternally alters one's destiny.

Which is why: when I see you, la belle France, rejoicing breaks my mind.

A LETTER FROM THE ARTIST

———

I am grateful to say life has taken me on a unique journey of excitement, beauty, humor, grief, and much more. I hope you were able to see and feel the fullness of life running through these pages. I believe life and art are married, and I believe art is for all of us.

I've noticed the poets, musicians, and artists whom I greatly admire build their work around the beauty and ephemeral nature of life. How, if we are but a wisp of vapor, a thread in time, the syllable of a single rhyme, what are we to do with this one precious life?

The answer comes down to "it all".

So then, my new friend: it is your turn. Take your pen, brushes, lyrics, music, and learn to believe. Move into that inner sanctuary and heal. Then write the world you *know* we're all meant to see. We're in this together.

All my kindness, color, and joy,

PAIGE D. LEHMANN

Made in the USA
Monee, IL
28 July 2023

1ecd9ebe-b40c-4959-8de8-d7a4d7e1d8d4R01